A Taste of LeCroissant

www.lecroissantcatering.com

*Sue!
May all your food adventures
be as fabulous as you are!
Kisses!
Chris Sanchez*

Copyright © 2013
LeCroissant Catering
Salt Lake City, Utah
www.lecroissantcatering.com

Locally designed and printed:
Artistic Printing
Salt Lake City, Utah

photography by: Dav.d Daniels
www.daviddanielsphotography.com

A Taste of
LeCroissant

from the creative team at
LeCroissant Catering

Acknowledgements

We express our deep gratitude to the following for their contributions, hard work, and dedication to this book: Chef Jane Hamilton, Nate Garrett, Kelly Lake, Stephanie Romero, Pat Slade, Christopher Sanchez, Becky Knight, Taylor Lake, Joesph Bradford, Chris Lake, Bethany Loveless, and all the others that helped to compile, organize, and edit this cookbook. Our thanks also to our incredible photographer Dav.d Daniels for his beautiful work. Also a special thanks to Mountain Land Design for allowing us the use of their exquisite kitchens.

about us

LeCroissant Catering is more than a full-service catering company. We create relationships with our clients. We enjoy getting to know our clients - their dreams, and passions. We pride ourselves on making our clients' dreams a reality by consistently partnering with them each and every step of the way. We closely monitor the latest trends in food, style, art, and entertainment. And we always make sure no matter how big or small an event may be…it's our job to pay attention to detail.

For corporations, we understand brand image, and attaining goals, and we strive to deliver signature style and quality. In any economic environment, we work within your budget to ensure a seamless and spectacular event.

Founded in 1995, LeCroissant Catering has continually grown to what it is today. Pat Slade, owner, began working as a caterer in St George, UT over 40 years ago. She then moved to Salt Lake City and began her own business, Pat's Weddings. John and Kelly Lake, partners and owners today, have worked with Pat for over 30 years. Even before Pat became a caterer she and her brother John were in the food service business, working for their father at the family owned restaurant The Hungry Guy, which was for many years located on 1300 East near the University of Utah Campus.

Our capabilities and reputation have grown along with our passionate and brilliant staff. We are a collection of dedicated and caring individuals who are full of energy, ambition and professionalism. Our team works together each day to create incredible events. At LeCroissant Catering, we love to cook and we love to celebrate! Our philosophy is to create glorious food while creating incredible memories and unforgettable experiences. We do not believe that it is unusual to have life changing experiences while enjoying fabulous food, and we have made it our mission to see that it happens more frequently.

This cookbook is dedicated to all of our friends, family, incredible staff, and our clients who have all helped us to become who we are today.
Thank you!

contents

Introduction	viii
Desserts	1
Appetizers	27
Soups	43
Salads & Dressings	55
Entrees	77
Side Dishes	103
Muffins, Breads & Spreads	123
Beverages & Cocktails	143
Kitchen Conversions	158
Index	159

introduction

The recipes in this book come from many places–friends, family, and things we've developed in the LeCroissant kitchens. All of us have been inspired by amazing meals, fun travels, other cooks, great chefs, and even by the occasional food dream. Thanks to everyone who has played a part in this collection!

We haven't come across many recipes that we haven't changed at least a little. In that spirit, please use these recipes as a starting point, change anything you'd like, and if you come up with something especially wonderful, share it with us!

desserts

We decided to start with desserts because you should always start with dessert.

"…life is uncertain, eat dessert first"

-Ernestine Ulme

Best Ever Cheesecake

Fudge Brownies

Chocolate Chip Cookies

Our Famous Sugar Cookies
with Raspberry Buttercream Frosting

Waffle Brownies

Banana Cake

desserts

Lemon Pound Cake

Kelly's Chocolate Cake
with Chocolate Fudge Frosting

Vanilla Cake

Texas Fudge Cake

White Chocolate Coconut Fudge

LeCroissant Dessert Crepes
with Chocolate Sauce & Vanilla Brandy Sauce

a few notes before you start...

The most important thing to remember is that dessert should be fun! Even if you make a mistake, you can almost always figure out some way to salvage your project—undercook your brownies? Well, just call them "Extra Fudgy Brownies", scoop them into a bowl and top them with ice cream. Drop or break your cake layers? Break them into bite sized pieces and layer them in a bowl with whipped cream and fruit. You've created a trifle! If you've over-baked your cookies, cool them and crumble them up for ice cream topping. Ice cream really will fix almost anything.

***Most importantly, have fun, be creative,
and eat sweets!***

best ever cheesecake

32 ounces	cream cheese, softened
1 ⅓ cup	granulated sugar
4	eggs, room temperature
¼ cup	sour cream
1 teaspoon	vanilla
1	crumb crust, pressed into bottom of 9" springform pan

Preheat oven to 300 degrees. Beat cream cheese until smooth. Add sugar, vanilla and sour cream. Add eggs one at a time just until combined. Don't overmix! Pour into springform pan. Bake at 300 degrees for about 1 hour or until cheesecake is firmly set around edges and slightly soft in the center. Remove from oven, cool and then chill completely before removing from pan and cutting.

helpful hint:

Store cheesecake in freezer. 30 minutes before cutting, remove from freezer. Cut into desired serving size with 12" chef's knife, wiping blade between cuts.

Cheesecake is done when the outer ⅔ of the cheesecake is set but the inner 1 ½ to 2 inches still is a little bit soft and jiggly. If your cheesecake has puffed up while baking, your oven was just a little bit too warm. Don't worry about it-it will fall as it cools. If it cracks, either frost the cheesecake with a little whipped cream or put your favorite fruit topping over it. It's still going to be delicious!

fudge brownies

½ cup	butter, melted
⅓ cup	good quality cocoa
1 cup	sugar
½ cup	flour
2	eggs, lightly beaten
1 teaspoon	vanilla, best quality
pinch	salt
2 ounces (⅓ cup)	coarsely chopped semi-sweet chocolate*
	*use your favorite chocolate bar for this

    Preheat oven to 350 degrees. In medium mixing bowl, combine flour, sugar and salt. Whisk to combine. Stir cocoa into warm, melted butter. (This step will help develop the flavor of the cocoa.) Gently combine flour mixture, butter mixture, eggs, vanilla and chocolate. Stir just until combined. Pour into greased and floured or parchment lined 9" square pan. Bake for 20-25 minutes. Let cool for as long as you can wait before cutting into 2" pieces. Yield approximately 16 brownies.

    Brownies are done when the outer edges (about 2-3 inches) feel firm and the center isn't quite firm. This is mostly a matter of personal preference. If you like gooey brownies, you'll want to have them very cool before you cut them.

chocolate chip cookies

1 pound	butter, softened
1 ounce	cream cheese, softened
1 ½ cups	granulated sugar
2 cups	brown sugar
½ teaspoon	salt
1 ½ teaspoons	baking soda (use just a little more if you're baking at sea level)
1 ½ teaspoons	vanilla, best quality
6 cups	flour, divided
4 cups	chocolate chips

This dough is very stiff, so if you have a stand mixer this is a great place to use it. Cream together butter, cream cheese, sugars, salt and baking soda until fluffy, about 2 minutes. With mixer running add eggs. Turn off mixture and stir down the sides of your bowl. Toss chocolate chips with ¼ cup flour. Stir remaining flour into butter mixture to combine. Stir in the chocolate chips you've mixed with the flour.

Drop cookie batter by tablespoonful onto parchment lined baking sheet. Bake at 350 degrees until edges are golden and middle is still soft, about 8-12 minutes depending on size of cookies. Don't over bake!

Yield about 3 ½ dozen nice sized cookies or about 6 dozen small cookies.

Note: this dough stores very well in the freezer. Scoop the dough into desired size cookie balls, freeze, and then keep in zipper freezer bag up to 3 months. If baking frozen, add about 2 minutes onto your baking time.

For a special treat, dip one half of each cooled cookie into melted chocolate. Let chocolate harden before serving.

our famous sugar cookies

1 pound	butter, softened
2 ounces	cream cheese, softened (do not substitute low fat cream cheese)
3 cups	granulated sugar
½ cup	brown sugar
½ teaspoon	salt
1 ½ teaspoons	baking soda
3	eggs
1 ½ teaspoons	vanilla, best quality
1/16 teaspoon	almond extract
6 cups	all purpose flour

Preheat oven to 350 degrees. Using a stand mixer, cream together butter, cream cheese, sugars, salt, and baking soda. Add eggs and scrape down mixing bowl. Add extracts. Blend well then add flour until combined. Don't overmix!

Drop by tablespoonsful onto parchment lined baking sheet. Bake for 8-12 minutes depending on size of cookies. Cookies are done when edges are golden and center is still soft.

Frost cookies with Raspberry Buttercream Frosting

Most cookies are done when the edges are golden and the center isn't quite set. Generally it's a good idea to take the cookies out of the oven just about 1 ½ minutes before you think they're finished baking.

raspberry buttercream frosting

2 cups	softened butter (no substitutions)
4 cups	powdered sugar
2 teaspoons	best quality vanilla
2 tablespoons	raspberry brandy

Beat all ingredients together until very light and fluffy, about 7 minutes.

waffle brownies

½ cup	butter, melted
⅓ cup	cocoa
4	eggs
1 ½ cups	granulated sugar
2 cups	all purpose flour
½ teaspoon	baking powder
½ teaspoon	salt

In medium mixing bowl, stir all ingredients together until well blended. Drop by tablespoonfuls into hot, greased waffle iron. Cook approximately 1 minute or until done.

Frost Waffle Brownies with Chocolate Fudge Frosting
(Kelly's Favorite Frosting)

chocolate fudge frosting (kelly's favorite frosting)

¾ cup	butter
⅓ cup	heavy cream
10 ounces	semi-sweet chocolate, coarsely chopped (use your favorite chocolate for this)
¾ cup	sour cream
3 cups	powdered sugar
1 teaspoon	vanilla

Place chocolate in a mixing bowl or in the work bowl of your food processor. Bring butter and cream to a boil. Pour all at once over chocolate. Let stand 1 minute then stir until melted. Cool slightly.

Stir in sour cream and vanilla, then powdered sugar. Beat until frosting reaches desired consistency. If necessary, add a few drops of hot water to thin the frosting or a bit more powdered sugar to make it more stiff. These adjustments might be necessary depending on the cake you're frosting and how humid your kitchen is.

banana cake

This is one of our absolute favorites! It also works well for very rich banana muffins.

1 ½ cups	butter, softened
1 ½ cups	granulated sugar
½ teaspoon	salt
1 teaspoon	baking soda
3	eggs
1 ½ cups	mashed, over ripe bananas
2 ⅔ cups	all purpose flour
½ cup	buttermilk
1 teaspoon	vanilla

Preheat oven to 350 degrees. In mixing bowl, cream together butter, sugar, salt and baking soda until fluffy. Add eggs, one at a time. Stir in bananas, then flour, scraping bottom of the bowl frequently. Add buttermilk and vanilla. Beat for 1 minute. Divide batter between 3 – greased and floured 9" cake pans. Bake for 20-25 minutes, or until cake tests done. Let stand 10 minutes before removing from pan to cool completely.

Frost Banana Cake with Cream Cheese Frosting

cream cheese frosting

1 pound	softened butter
1 pound	softened cream cheese
8 ½ cups (2 pounds)	powdered sugar
1 ½ teaspoons	vanilla

In large mixing bowl, beat all ingredients together until smooth and fluffy. If necessary, add milk 1 teaspoon at a time until desired consistency is achieved. This will make enough frosting to generously frost and fill a 3 layer cake.

lemon pound cake

This is a fairly traditional pound cake, which means most of the leavening comes from the way you mix the cake. You'll bake this in a tube pan-a pan that looks like a giant, straight sided donut with a removable bottom. Prepare the pan carefully with grease and flour. Make sure you pay attention to the center of the pan when you're preparing it.

After baking, let the cake stand for 10 minutes, then loosen the sides. Very gently flip the cake pan over onto a cooling rack or serving platter. Let stand a few more minutes, then jiggle the pan until the cake slides out. It might sound a bit complicated, but this cake is worth it! An extra minute or two before you put the batter in the pan will pay off when it's time to remove the cake.

1 cup	butter, softened
2 cups	sugar
½ teaspoon	baking soda
½ teaspoon	salt
3	eggs, room temperature
1 cup	buttermilk
2 tablespoons	fresh lemon juice*
2 tablespoons	fresh lemon zest*

*Plan on about 3 lemons. Zest them all-you'll need it for the cake and the glaze. After you've removed the zest, juice the lemons. For the cake and glaze you'll want a total of about half a cup of fresh juice.

Preheat oven to 350 degrees. Cream the butter, sugar, baking soda and salt together, stopping to scrape down the bowl periodically. Cream the mixture for about 3 minutes, or until lightened in color. Gradually add the eggs. Stir in the flour alternately with the buttermilk, beginning and ending with the flour. Very gently add the lemon juice and zest. Pour into prepared tube pan (see notes at beginning of recipe) and bake for 15 minutes. Carefully turn pan ¼ turn. Continue baking another 30-40 minutes or until cake tests done. Cool 10 minutes, then turn pan over onto serving dish or cooling rack. This is especially delicious accompanied by fresh berries.

lemon glaze

½ cup	melted butter
3 cups	powdered sugar
⅓ cup	warm lemon juice, divided
1 teaspoon	lemon zest

Place powdered sugar in a mixing bowl and whisk gently to break up any lumps. Beat in butter and half the lemon juice. Gradually stir in remaining lemon juice and lemon zest. Pour warm or room temperature glaze over hot Lemon Pound Cake.

variations:

*Replace lemon juice and zest with any citrus.
Lime and Blood Orange are both lovely!*

kelly's favorite

This is one of my favorite cakes. It's a little softer than a lot of other cakes and is very moist. If you prefer your chocolate a little less dark, simply use a milk chocolate frosting and just frost the middle and top of the cake.

If you're like me and can never get enough chocolate, spread a good ganache (really this is just chocolate melted with a bit of cream) between the layers and finish the cake with your favorite chocolate frosting. Whipped cream is wonderful with this cake, too.

kelly's chocolate cake

1 cup	boiling water
¾ cup	good quality cocoa
¾ cup	milk
¼ cup	sour cream (not reduced fat)
½ cup	softened butter
2 cups	granulated sugar
¼ teaspoon	salt
1 ½ teaspoons	baking soda
3	eggs
1 teaspoon	vanilla
1 ¾ cups	all purpose flour

Preheat oven to 350 degrees. Combine boiling water and cocoa in a small bowl or measuring cup. Set aside to cool. Combine milk and sour cream in another small bowl and set aside. In large mixing bowl, cream butter with sugar, salt and baking soda until fluffy. Scrape down the sides and bottom of the bowl. Add eggs one at a time until combined. Add vanilla. Add flour alternately with milk mixture until combined. Stir in cooled cocoa mixture. Divide batter between 3 parchment lined 9" cake pans. Bake for 20-25 minutes. Cake will be done when a few crumbs stick to a toothpick inserted in the center of the cake. Let stand 10 minutes before removing to a cooling rack. These cake layers will be soft and somewhat delicate.

Frost and fill as desired-Kelly's Chocolate Frosting from page 13 is a great choice.

vanilla cake

1 ½ cups	softened butter
1 ¼ cups	granulated sugar
½ teaspoon	salt
¼ teaspoon	baking soda
1 tablespoon	baking powder
1 ½ teaspoons	vanilla
4	eggs
3 cups	flour
⅔ cup	milk
3 tablespoons	sour cream

Preheat oven to 350 degrees. Beat butter, sugar, salt, baking soda and baking powder together until fluffy. This will take about 3 minutes in a stand mixer. Scrape down sides of bowl. Add remaining ingredients and mix for another 3 minutes on medium speed. Divide batter between 3 greased and floured 9" cake pans. Bake for about 20 minutes or until cake just tests done. Don't overbake! Remove from pans and cool.

Frost cake with Raspberry Buttercream Frosting found on page 11.

texas fudge cake

1 cup	butter
1 cup	water
⅓ cup	cocoa (if you love chocolate, increase the cocoa to ½ cup)
2 cups	flour
2 cups	granulated sugar
½ teaspoon	salt
1 teaspoon	baking soda
2	eggs
½ cup	buttermilk
1 teaspoon	vanilla

Preheat oven to 350 degrees. Combine butter, water and cocoa in small pan or microwave safe bowl. Bring ingredients to a boil. Set aside to cool. In mixing bowl, whisk together flour, sugar, salt and baking soda. Make sure all the ingredients are well-distributed. Add cocoa mixture, eggs, buttermilk and vanilla. Stir to combine. Pour into 9" x 13" pan that has been sprayed with non-stick cooking spray. Bake for approximately 25 minutes or until it tests done. Cool completely before frosting.

texas fudge frosting

⅓ cup	whole milk
¼ cup	cocoa
½ cup	butter
1 teaspoon	vanilla
3 ½ cups	powdered sugar

In heavy pan or microwave safe bowl, bring milk, cocoa and butter to a boil. Beat in powdered sugar and vanilla. While still warm, pour over Texas Fudge Cake.

white chocolate coconut fudge

1 can	sweetened condensed milk (not evaporated milk)
4 cups	white chocolate chips
1 cup	shredded coconut
½ teaspoon	coconut extract

Begin by lining an 8" pan with plastic wrap, allowing plastic wrap to hang over side of pan. In a medium sized microwave safe bowl, heat sweetened condensed milk to almost boiling (about 3 minutes), then stir in white chocolate chips. If chocolate chips are not completely melted at this point, return to microwave for 20 seconds at a time until melted. Stir in coconut and coconut extract.

Finally, spread fudge over plastic wrap. Cover and refrigerate until firm, then cut into squares.

LeCroissant dessert crepes

5	eggs, room temperature
4 cups	whole milk, divided
3 generous cups	flour
¼ cup	granulated sugar
1 teaspoon	vanilla
2 drops	almond extract
½ cup	melted butter or margarine

Combine eggs, 2 ½ cups milk, flour, sugar and extracts. Beat until completely smooth. Stir in melted butter or margarine until just combined, then remaining milk. Let stand 30 minutes before cooking.

In a non-stick 8" frying pan over medium heat, pour in a scant ¼ cup of batter, swirling as you pour. When bubbles start to form and edges are slightly crisp, flip crepe over. Let cook another 30 seconds then remove from pan. Roll them up and top with your favorite fillings such as fruit, pudding, or whipped cream! Makes about 50 crepes.

Top Crepes with delicious sauces, recipes on page 26.

crepe toppings

chocolate sauce

¾ cup	cocoa
1 cup	light corn syrup
½ cup	heavy cream
2 tablespoons	butter
pinch	salt
1 teaspoon	vanilla

Combine all ingredients except vanilla in heavy medium saucepan. Bring to a gentle boil and cook, stirring, for 5 minutes. Remove from heat and stir in vanilla.

vanilla brandy sauce

2 cups	granulated sugar
2 cups	heavy cream
½ cup	butter
1 tablespoon	brandy
2 teaspoons	vanilla

In heavy saucepan, combine sugar, cream and butter. Stir over medium heat until sugar is dissolved and butter is melted. Do not boil. Remove from heat and stir in flavorings.

variation:

Replace brandy with light rum or ½ teaspoon of rum extract

appetizers

"Food is not about impressing people. It's about making them feel comfortable."

-Ina Garten

Spicy Artichoke Dip

Dill Dip

Cherry Cheese Ball

appetizers

Traditional Bruschetta Topping

Baked Brie in Puff Pastry

Trio of Salsas
Jicama and Cilantro, Traditional Red & Tropical Fruit

Baked Flour Tortilla Chips

Roasted Tomato Hummus

Pasilla Caper Hummus

spicy artichoke dip

16 ounces	cream cheese, softened
½ cup	diced, canned green chilies
¼ cup	diced, canned jalapeños
1 cup	shredded mozzarella
1 (16 ounce) can	artichoke hearts, drained
½ cup	shredded parmesan

Mix all ingredients except parmesan. Place in 9" round lightly greased casserole pan. Sprinkle top with parmesan. Bake at 325 degrees until golden brown and bubbly. Serve with chips or sliced breads.

dill dip

1 cup	mayonnaise
1 cup	sour cream
½ cup	fresh dill, finely chopped or 2 tablespoons dried dill
1 tablespoon	fresh parsley, finely chopped or 1 teaspoon dried parsley
1 tablespoon	finely chopped green onion
	salt to taste

Combine all ingredients. Let refrigerate for one hour prior to serving. Serve with fresh vegetables.

cherry cheese ball

16 ounces	cream cheese, softened (NOT reduced fat)
⅓ cup	powdered sugar
¾ cup	shredded coconut (unsweetened)
¼ cup	maraschino cherries, chopped
1 tablespoon	juice from maraschino cherries
⅛ teaspoon	almond extract
¼ teaspoon	vanilla
1 cup	chopped pecans

Lightly toast pecans in 300 degree oven about 8 minutes or until nuts are barely fragrant. Set aside to cool. Beat softened cream cheese until fluffy. Gradually whip in remaining ingredients except pecans. Form into ball using clean, damp hands. Roll in chopped nuts and refrigerate until set, at least 3 hours. Serve with sliced apples or crackers.

traditional bruschetta topping

3	large fresh tomatoes, chopped and seeded
2 cloves	garlic, finely minced
1	green onion, chopped
2 tablespoons	fresh basil, chopped
2 teaspoons	olive oil
	salt and pepper to taste

In small serving bowl, combine tomatoes, garlic, onion, basil, olive oil, salt and pepper. Let stand for 30 minutes at room temperature before serving. Serve with Crostini (olive oil toasted sliced breads) or crackers.

baked brie in puff pastry

2 pound	wheel of Brie
1 package	frozen puff pastry, thawed but still cold
½ cup	favorite preserves (we love fig or raspberry)
	flour for work area

Preheat oven to 400 degrees. Cut Brie in half horizontally. Spread preserves on bottom half to within 1" of edge. Replace top. Place 1 sheet of puff pastry on lightly floured work surface. Center Brie on pastry sheet. Place second sheet of pastry on top of Brie, cutting off excess edges. Bring bottom sheet of pastry over top, crimping edges to create a seal. Transfer to baking sheet. Bake for 30 minutes, or until lightly browned. Let stand for 10 minutes before removing to serving platter. Serve with sliced breads or crackers.

trio of salsas

jicama and cilantro salsa

1 cup	fresh cilantro
1 tablespoon	fresh mint
1 large	jalapeño
1 teaspoon	sugar
3 tablespoons	lime juice
2 pounds	jicama, peeled and coarsely chopped
	salt to taste

Combine cilantro, mint, jalapeño, jicama, sugar and lime juice in food processor. Pulse until finely chopped. Chill for at least 2 hours. Add salt to taste.

traditional red salsa

2 cups	chopped fresh tomatoes or 16 ounces good quality canned diced tomatoes
½ cup	chopped white onion
2 to 4	fresh jalapeños, depending on desired heat
	juice of 1 lime
⅛ teaspoon	dried oregano, crumbled
1 tablespoon	fresh cilantro
	salt to taste

In small dry sauté pan, toast jalapeños until blackened on all sides. Cool, and then remove stems, skins and seeds. Place all ingredients in blender or food processor. Process until chunky but not too fine. Add salt to taste.

tropical fruit salsa

1	ripe mango, peeled and chopped
1	ripe papaya, peeled and chopped
2 cups	fresh pineapple, chopped
2	ripe kiwi fruit, peeled and chopped
¼ cup	red onion, finely diced
1	fresh jalapeño, finely diced
1 tablespoon	fresh mint or cilantro, chopped
	juice of 1 lime
	salt to taste

Combine all ingredients. Let stand at room temperature for 30 minutes. Add salt to taste.

baked flour tortilla chips

1　package uncooked flour tortillas
　　non-stick pan spray
　　salt,
　　cinnamon sugar or
　　shredded parmesan

    Cut raw tortillas into wedges. Separate and place on ungreased baking sheet. Spray tortilla wedges with non-stick pan spray. Turn over and spray second side. Sprinkle with choice of salt, cinnamon sugar or shredded parmesan. Bake at 375 degrees for about 5 minutes or until golden and crisp. Serve with choice of salsa.

roasted tomato hummus

1 cup	diced fresh tomatoes
3 tablespoons	olive oil, divided
⅛ teaspoon	coarse salt
1 (15 ounce) can	chickpeas or garbanzo beans, rinsed and drained
1 tablespoon	fresh flat leaf parsley
2 tablespoons	fresh lemon juice
1 clove	fresh garlic
	salt and pepper to taste

Toss diced tomatoes with 1 tablespoon olive oil and ⅛ teaspoon coarse salt in small mixing bowl. Place on sheet pan and bake at 400 degrees for 8-10 minutes or until softened and starting to color. In food processor, combine tomatoes with their liquid, chickpeas, remaining olive oil, parsley, lemon juice and garlic. Process until smooth. If necessary, add up to 2 tablespoons of water to obtain desired consistency.

pasilla caper hummus

1 (15 ounce) can	chickpeas or garbanzo beans, rinsed and drained
3 tablespoons	olive oil
2 to 3 tablespoons	water
2 tablespoons	fresh lime juice
½ teaspoon	fresh garlic
2	fresh pasilla peppers, stems and seeds removed
1 tablespoon	capers, rinsed and drained
¼ cup	fresh cilantro
	salt and pepper to taste

Place chickpeas, lime juice, olive oil, water, garlic, peppers, capers, cilantro and a large pinch of salt in food processor. Process until smooth. If too thick, add additional water. Season with salt and pepper to taste.

soups

"Worries go down better with soup."
-Jewish Proverb

Creamy Tomato Soup

Cream of Broccoli Soup

soups

Slow-Cooker White Chicken Chili

Busy Day Beef Stew

Potato Bacon Soup

creamy tomato soup

2 tablespoons	butter
2 tablespoons	flour
½	yellow onion, diced
½ cup	white wine
2 cups	tomato juice
1 cup	canned diced tomatoes
1 (16 ounce) can	chicken or vegetable stock
1 cup	heavy cream
	salt and black pepper, to taste
2 tablespoons	fresh basil, finely chopped

    Heat butter on medium heat and sauté onions until they begin to sweat. Gradually stir in the flour to make a roux and cook for about a minute. Deglaze with white wine and let reduce until almost dry. Add tomato puree and cook for 1-2 minutes. Whisk in stock and bring to a boil. Turn heat to low and simmer for at least 20 minutes. Add heavy cream and season to taste with salt and pepper. Serve hot with fresh chopped basil garnish.

cream of broccoli soup

2 pounds	broccoli
1 ½ cups	diced onions
1 cup	diced celery
	water
2 tablespoons	chicken base
2 to 3	bay leaves
3 cups	cream
3 cups	milk
	salt and pepper to taste
½ teaspoon	worcestershire sauce

for roux:

¾ cup	butter
⅔ cup	flour

Trim ends of broccoli. Separate stems from florets. Place broccoli stems, onions, celery and bay leaves in large heavy pan. Cover with water. Add chicken base. Bring to boil and simmer until vegetables are soft. Remove bay leaves. Puree vegetables until smooth.

To make roux, melt butter in saucepan over medium heat. Add flour and stir, cooking, until flour taste is cooked out, about 1-2 minutes. Add cream and milk to vegetable mixture and return to a boil. Whisk in roux until soup reaches desired consistency. Stir in worcestershire and salt and pepper to taste. Divide the broccoli florets into very small pieces. Stir into soup and cook until broccoli is bright green and slightly softened. Makes about 4-6 servings.

slow-cooker white chicken chili

2	jalapeños, seeded and minced
1	poblano pepper, seeded and diced
2	yellow onions, diced
5 cloves	garlic, minced
3 (15 ounce) cans	Great Northern white beans, drained and rinsed
2	boneless chicken breasts
1	boneless chicken thigh
3 tablespoons	dried basil
1 ½ teaspoons	cayenne pepper
3	tomatoes, diced
2 ½ cups	shredded monterey jack cheese
	salt to taste
½ cup	fresh cilantro, chopped

In a slow cooker, add the jalapeños, onions, garlic, and beans and place chicken on top. Top the chicken with basil and cayenne. Cover and slow cook on low for 6-8 hours or until chicken is fork-tender. Remove the chicken and shred with a fork before adding back into the slow cooker along with the tomatoes and cheese. Cover and cook for an additional 15 minutes until the cheese is melted all the way. Season to taste with salt and more cayenne pepper if desired. Serve hot garnished with tortilla chips and garnished with fresh cilantro.

busy day beef stew

2 pounds	cubed stew meat
¼ cup	flour
1 teaspoon	salt
	pepper, to taste
2 tablespoons	vegetable oil
5	carrots, cut into 1" dice
5	potatoes, cut into 1" dice
1 medium	turnip, diced
½ cup	sliced celery
1 large	tomato, peeled and diced
½ cup	red wine
2 cans	cream of mushroom soup
1 package	dry onion soup mix
4 cups	water

Preheat oven to 400 degrees. Dredge meat in flour, salt and pepper, then toss with oil in 3 quart casserole dish. Bake uncovered for 30 minutes, stirring once. Add remaining ingredients. Cover and bake at 375 degrees for 2-3 hours.

potato bacon soup

2 tablespoons	butter
6 strips	bacon, chopped
1	yellow onion, diced
½ cup	carrot, diced
½ cup	celery, diced
5 cloves	garlic, minced
2 tablespoons	flour
½ cup	white wine
1 (16 ounce) can	chicken or vegetable stock
4 large	russet potatoes, peeled and cut into ¾" cubes
1 cup	milk
1 cup	heavy cream
1	bay leaf
1 tablespoon	fresh rosemary, minced
1 tablespoon	fresh thyme, minced
	salt and black pepper, to taste

Heat butter over medium heat in a stockpot. Add chopped bacon and cook until it starts to get crispy. Add the onions, celery, and carrots and cook for about 5 minutes, or until they start to caramelize, then add the garlic and sauté until it's lightly brown, about 1 minute. Gradually add the flour while stirring to make a roux and cook for about one minute. Deglaze with white wine, stir, and cook until reduced and the alcohol is cooked out. Whisk in the stock and then add the potatoes. Bring the soup to a boil and then turn the heat to low. Simmer for 10-15 minutes, until potatoes are tender and cooked through. Add the milk, cream and herbs and continue to simmer for another 5 minutes. Season with salt and pepper to taste. Remove the bay leaf and serve hot with rolls or bread.

salads & dressings

"To remember a successful salad is generally to remember a successful dinner; at all events, the perfect dinner necessarily includes the perfect salad."

George Ellwanger

salads

Spinach Mandarin Salad

Shrimp Macaroni Salad

Fiesta Fruit Salad

Salad Nicoise

Potato Salad with Dill Dressing

Caprese Salad

Chopped Salad

Black Bean, Jicama & Grilled Corn Salad

& dressings

Raspberry Poppy Seed Dressing

Balsamic Vinaigrette

Lemon Vinaigrette

Creamy Ranch Dressing

Creamy Italian Vinaigrette

spinach mandarin salad

8 ounces	slivered almonds
2 tablespoons	sugar
½ head	red leaf lettuce
½ bunch	spinach
½ head	iceberg lettuce
1 basket	fresh strawberries, hulled and sliced
2 small cans	mandarin oranges, drained
½	cucumber, sliced

Slowly stir almonds in sugar over low to medium heat until caramelized. Cool in a single layer on a sheet of wax paper. Wash and tear all greens. Combine salad ingredients. Serve with your favorite dressing.

shrimp macaroni salad

3 cups	cooked pasta, cooled to room temperature (macaroni or similar tube shaped pasta)
½ pound	cooked salad shrimp, chilled
1 cup	mayonnaise
¼ cup	red onion, diced
¼ cup	celery, diced
	salt and pepper to taste

Combine all ingredients. Let rest in refrigerator for 2-4 hours before serving. If salad is too dry, add additional mayonnaise.

fiesta fruit salad

2 cups	fresh pineapple, cut into bite sized pieces
1 cup	fresh mango, cut into bite sized pieces
2 cups	fresh berries (sliced strawberries, blueberries, blackberries, etc.)
1 cup	fresh melon (honeydew, cantaloupe or watermelon) cut into bite sized pieces
2	fresh kiwi, peeled and sliced
¼ cup	toasted coconut, reserved

for dressing:

½ cup	orange juice
¼ cup	granulated sugar
2 tablespoons	light rum or coconut rum
1 teaspoon	vanilla

In serving bowl, toss all fruit together except for toasted coconut. In a separate bowl combine juice, sugar, rum and vanilla. Toss with cut fruit. Let stand 30 minutes. Top with toasted coconut and serve.

salad nicoise

2 (8 ounces each)	grilled tuna steaks or 2-3 cans of tuna
6	hard boiled eggs, chilled, peeled and quartered
10 small	new red potatoes (each about 2 inches in diameter, about 1 ¼ pounds total), scrubbed and quartered
	salt and freshly ground black pepper
2 medium heads	boston lettuce or butter lettuce, leaves washed, dried, and torn into bite-sized pieces
3 small	ripe tomatoes, cored and cut into eighths
1 small	red onion, sliced very thin
8 ounces	green beans, stem ends trimmed and each bean halved crosswise
¼ cup	olives (preferably nicoise olives)
2 tablespoons	capers, rinsed

for lemon vinaigrette

½ cup	lemon juice
¾ cup	extra-virgin olive oil
1 medium	shallot, minced
1 tablespoon	minced fresh thyme leaves
2 tablespoons	minced fresh basil leaves
2 teaspoons	minced fresh oregano leaves
1 teaspoon	dijon mustard
	salt and freshly ground black pepper

Salads & Dressings

Marinate tuna steaks in a little olive oil for an hour. Heat a large skillet on medium high heat, or place on a hot grill. Cook the steaks 2 to 3 minutes on each side until cooked through. Cool completely.

Bring potatoes and 4 quarts cold water to boil in a large pot. Add 1 tablespoon salt and cook until potatoes are tender, 5 to 8 minutes. Transfer potatoes to a medium bowl with a slotted spoon (do not discard boiling water). Toss warm potatoes with ¼ cup vinaigrette; set aside to cool.

While potatoes are cooking, toss lettuce with ¼ cup vinaigrette in large bowl until coated. Arrange bed of lettuce on a serving platter, cut tuna into ½-inch thick slices, coat with vinaigrette. Mound the tuna in center of lettuce. Toss tomatoes, red onion, 3 tablespoons vinaigrette, and salt and pepper to taste in bowl; arrange tomato onion mixture on the lettuce bed. Arrange reserved potatoes in a mound at edge of lettuce bed.

Return reserved potato water to a boil; add 1 tablespoon salt and the green beans. Cook until tender but crisp, 3 to 5 minutes. Drain beans, transfer into a bowl of ice water, and let stand until cool, about 30 seconds; dry beans well. Toss beans, 3 tablespoons vinaigrette, and salt and pepper to taste; arrange in a mound at edge of lettuce bed.

Arrange hard boiled eggs, and olives in mounds on the lettuce bed. Drizzle eggs with remaining 2 tablespoons of dressing, sprinkle entire salad with capers (if using), and serve immediately.

potato salad with dill dressing

5 pounds	potatoes, diced
12	hard boiled eggs, peeled
½ cup	finely diced onion
1 cup	dill relish or 2 cups finely chopped pickles
2 cups	mayonnaise
1 tablespoon	dill weed
	salt and pepper to taste
1 ½ teaspoons	red wine vinegar
½ teaspoon	mustard

Bring a large pot of salted water to a boil. Add potatoes and cook until tender but still firm, about 15 minutes. Drain, cool, and chill. Finely chop eggs and combine with all remaining ingredients. Stir in potatoes. Taste and adjust seasonings.

caprese salad

1 pound	fresh mozzarella, cut into ¼" slices
6	vine ripened tomatoes (preferably heirloom) cut into ¼" slices
1 medium bunch	fresh basil (about 20 leaves)
2 tablespoons	olive oil
2 teaspoons	balsamic vinegar
	sea salt and pepper to taste

Alternate slices of tomato, basil and mozzarella on serving platter. Sprinkle with olive oil, balsamic vinegar, salt and pepper. Serve immediately at room temperature.

chopped salad

3	romaine lettuce hearts, chopped
½	english cucumber, cubed
½ cup	pitted kalamata olives, roughly chopped
¼ cup	sweet onion, minced
½ cup	red pepper, small dice
2	green onions, chopped
½ cup	feta cheese, crumbled
1 handful	mint leaves, roughly torn

Combine all ingredients in a bowl, finish with your choice of dressing.

black bean, jicama & grilled corn salad

2 cups	corn (fresh or canned)
5 tablespoons	extra-virgin olive oil, divided
2 (15 ounce) cans	black beans, rinsed, drained
1 cup	jicama, peeled and diced
1/3 cup	thinly sliced green onions
1/3 cup	chopped fresh cilantro
1/4 cup (packed)	chopped fresh basil
3 tablespoons	fresh lime juice
2 tablespoons	orange juice
2 1/2 teaspoons	lime zest
1/4 teaspoon	ground cumin

Blacken corn on dry skillet or frying pan, stirring occasionally. Let cool, then place in bowl. Add black beans, jicama, green onions, cilantro, and basil. Whisk lime juice, orange juice, lime peel, cumin, and remaining 4 tablespoons oil in small bowl. Mix dressing into bean salad. Season generously with salt and pepper. Cover and chill. Let stand at room temperature 1 hour before serving.

raspberry poppy seed dressing

1 ½ cups	vegetable oil
⅔ cup	cider vinegar or ⅓ cup white vinegar plus ⅓ cup red wine vinegar
2 tablespoons	diced yellow onion
2 tablespoons	diced green onion
2 teaspoons	salt
2 teaspoons	dry mustard
½ cup	sugar
½ cup	fresh or frozen raspberries
2 tablespoons	poppy seeds

Combine all ingredients in blender. Blend until creamy. Store in refrigerator for up to 1 week.

cranberry dressing

(great for the holidays!)

Make as above, substituting ¾ cup whole berry cranberry sauce for the berries.

balsamic vinaigrette

¼ cup	balsamic vinegar
1 teaspoon	dijon mustard
¾ cup	good quality olive oil
½ teaspoon	black pepper
1 teaspoon	salt

Combine all ingredients except olive oil in glass mixing bowl. Very slowly whisk in olive oil until combined and slightly thickened. Store tightly covered.

lemon vinaigrette

1 ¼ cups	lemon juice
1 teaspoon	lemon zest
2 cups	olive oil
2 medium	shallots
2 teaspoons	thyme
1 tablespoon	basil
1 teaspoon	oregano
2 teaspoons	dijon mustard
¼ cup	mayonnaise
1 teaspoon	salt
½ teaspoon	pepper

Combine all ingredients except olive oil in blender. Add olive oil in a slow drizzle to emulsify.

creamy ranch dressing

4 cups	buttermilk
4 cups	mayonnaise
2 teaspoons	salt
2 teaspoons	onion powder
1 ½ teaspoons	black pepper
1 ½ teaspoons	garlic, minced
2 tablespoons	parsley, chopped

In a blender, combine all ingredients. Pulse till creamy. Cover and refrigerate for 30 minutes before serving.

creamy italian vinaigrette

½ cup	mayonnaise
⅓ cup	red wine vinegar
2 tablespoons	olive oil
1 teaspoon	granulated sugar
¼ cup	grated Parmesan
1 clove	garlic, minced
⅛ teaspoon	dried oregano
⅛ teaspoon	dried basil
½ teaspoon	dried parsley
1 tablespoon	fresh lemon juice
½ teaspoon	black pepper
	salt to taste

In a blender, combine all ingredients until smooth.

entrees

"Cooking is like love, it should be entered into with abandon or not at all"

- Harriet Van Horne

Chicken Pot Pie

Campfire Trout

Southern Baked Chicken

Pork Tenderloin Tacos

Tuscan Chicken

entrees

Old Fashioned Pot Roast

Chicken Mushroom Alfredo

All Day Beef Stew

Baked Mac and Cheese

Southwestern Quiche

Mediterranean Quiche

White Trash Enchiladas

Celebration Waffles with Fruit Syrups

chicken pot pie

1 ½ pounds	boneless, skinless chicken breasts, cut into 1" pieces
1	yellow onion, diced
1 ½ cups	new red potatoes, cut into ¾" dice
1 ½ cups	carrots, sliced
½ cup	celery, sliced
½ cup	sliced fresh mushrooms
½ cup	fresh or frozen baby peas, thawed
¼ cup	olive oil
¼ cup	butter
⅓ cup	flour
½ teaspoon	granulated garlic
1 teaspoon	dried parsley
¼ teaspoon	dried tarragon
2 cups	chicken broth
1 cup	cream or half and half
	uncooked biscuits (use garlic cheese biscuit recipe from page 127)

Preheat oven to 400 degrees. In pan, heat olive oil and butter. Add chicken and onion, stirring until cooked through. Toss in flour. Cook, stirring for 3 minutes to make a roux. Stir in chicken broth, cream and seasonings. Mix until smooth. Add vegetables. Simmer for 20 minutes or until potatoes are softened, stirring frequently. Add mixture to oven safe dish. Top with uncooked biscuits.

Bake in preheated oven approximately 20 minutes or until biscuits are golden. Let stand 10 minutes before serving.

campfire trout

4	fresh trout, filleted with skin on
½ cup	butter
	non-stick cooking spray
1	lemon, sliced
	salt and pepper to taste
¼ cup	fresh parsley or dill

Heat heavy skillet or cast iron grill over medium high heat. Spray with non-stick spray. Season trout fillets with salt and pepper. Place trout in pan, then dot with butter. Cook 2-3 minutes. Carefully flip fillets. Place lemon slices and fresh herbs on top of trout. Continue cooking until trout flakes apart when lightly touched with a fork.

southern baked chicken

4	chicken breasts, bone in
4	chicken thighs, bone in
½ cup	milk
2 cups	flour
2 teaspoons	black pepper
1 tablespoon	seasoned salt
½ teaspoon	granulated garlic
½ teaspoon	granulated onion
1 cup	dried bread crumbs
	non-stick cooking spray

Preheat oven to 375 degrees. Combine flour, seasonings and bread crumbs. Dip chicken in milk, then dredge in seasoned flour mixture. Line a baking sheet with heavy aluminum foil. Spray very well with cooking spray. Place floured chicken on foil lined pan. Spray tops of chicken with cooking spray. Bake until golden and crispy. Chicken is done when internal temperature of thickest part of meat reaches 165 degrees, about 50 minutes.

Serve with Creamy Gravy and Mashed Potatoes.
Creamy Gravy recipe on page 86.

creamy gravy

2 tablespoons	butter
2 tablespoons	flour
½ cup	chicken stock
1 cup	milk
½ cup	heavy cream
½ teaspoon	garlic powder
1 teaspoon	onion powder
	salt and fresh ground black pepper

Heat the butter on medium heat in a medium saucepan. Add the flour to make a roux and cook for about a minute. Stir in the chicken stock, milk, and heavy cream. Add the garlic and onion powder and cook until thickened. Season to taste with salt and coarse ground black pepper.

pork tenderloin tacos

2 pounds	pork tenderloin, cut into ½" cubes
1 tablespoon	vegetable oil
½ cup	white onion, diced
½ teaspoon	granulated garlic
2 teaspoons	ground cumin
1 tablespoon	ground chili powder
¼ teaspoon	black pepper
1 (12 ounce) can	beer
½ cup	tomatoes, diced
	salt to taste
	corn or flour tortillas

condiments:

diced tomato
shredded lettuce or green cabbage
diced red onion

fresh limes, cut into wedges
salsa
shredded cheese

In a bowl, toss cubed pork tenderloin with oil. Heat sauté pan over medium high heat.

Add pork, taking care not to over crowd the pan. Sauté until pork is half cooked and browned.

Add onion, garlic, cumin, black pepper and chili powder to pan. Cook, stirring, until spices are fragrant and onion is softened. Add beer and tomatoes. Stir to combine and simmer for 15-20 minutes or until liquid is reduced. Add salt to taste. Heat tortillas until softened. Assemble tacos using your choice of condiments. Makes about 12 medium tacos.

tuscan chicken

for the chicken:

2 tablespoons	canola or vegetable oil
6	airline chicken breasts (boneless chicken breasts with the first wing section attached)
	salt and pepper

for the confit:

2 cups	grape or cherry tomatoes
1 (16 ounce) can	quartered artichoke hearts, drained
¼ cup + 2 tablespoons	white wine
4 tablespoons	olive oil
1	red onion, diced
4 cloves	garlic, minced
⅓ cup	capers, rinsed
⅓ cup	black or rinsed kalamata olives, pitted, halved
⅓ cup	green olives, pitted, halved

Preheat oven to 200 degrees. Put the tomatoes and artichoke hearts in a mixing bowl and toss in 2 tablespoons olive oil and ¼ cup white wine. Spread in an even layer on a foil-lined greased cookie sheet. Low roast for at least an hour or until tomatoes look sundried and have turned soft and sweet. The longer they are slow-roasted, the sweeter and softer they will be, and can be roasted up to 2-3 hours. Remove the tomatoes and artichokes from the pan and set aside.

    Preheat oven to 350 degrees. Generously season the skin side of the chicken breasts with salt and pepper. Heat the canola or vegetable oil in a sauté pan on high heat until it almost starts to smoke. Two or three at a time, place the chicken breasts skin side down in the pan and sear until the skin is golden brown and crispy. Transfer the breasts, skin side up, to a greased cookie sheet or roasting rack and finish in the oven for 5-10 minutes until the chicken reaches an internal temperature between 160-165 degrees.

    While the chicken is in the oven, heat the remaining two tablespoons. of olive oil in a medium saucepan on medium heat to begin finishing the confit sauce. Add the onions and sauté until translucent and then add the garlic and cook until lightly browned. Deglaze the pan with the remaining 2 tablespoons white wine and reduce until almost dry. Add the capers, olives, and tomato artichoke mixture and continue to cook, stirring occasionally until heated thoroughly. Top each chicken breast with about half a cup of confit and serve with pasta or polenta.

old fashioned pot roast

4-5 pounds	beef chuck roast, patted dry
2 tablespoons	vegetable oil
1	yellow onion, peeled and halved
1	carrot, rinsed and broken in half
1 cup	red wine
1 teaspoon	granulated garlic
1 teaspoon	black pepper
½ teaspoon	salt
1 cup	water

for gravy:

3 tablespoons	cornstarch
½ cup	cold water
	pan drippings from roast

Preheat oven to 300 degrees. Heat oil in large dutch oven with tight fitting lid. While oil is heating, season all sides of roast with salt and pepper. Brown the roast on all sides in the hot oil. Remove pan from heat. Add remaining ingredients. Place lid on pan, insuring tight fit. Bake in preheated oven for 4-6 hours, depending on size of roast. Roast is done when it shreds easily with a fork.

Remove meat, onions, and carrot from pan, reserving drippings in pan. Set meat aside to keep warm and discard vegetables. To make gravy, on stove top over medium high heat, add 1 cup of water to pan drippings. Bring to a boil, stirring to loosen any browned bits from bottom of pan. Dissolve cornstarch in cold water. Whisk into boiling pan drippings, stirring constantly. Taste and adjust salt and pepper. Serve with mashed potatoes.

chicken mushroom alfredo

3	boneless skinless chicken breasts, cut into bite sized pieces
3 tablespoons	butter
1 clove	garlic, minced
6	scallions, sliced
1 tablespoon	flour
⅓ cup	cream
½ cup	chicken broth
½ cup	shredded swiss cheese
¼ cup	grated parmesan
½ teaspoon	salt
	pepper to taste
1 cup	sliced mushrooms
2 tablespoons	fresh parsley
1 pound	bowtie pasta, cooked al dente

Toss cooked pasta with a little butter or olive oil and set aside. In a medium saucepan over medium heat sauté chicken, garlic, scallions, and mushrooms in butter until chicken is cooked through. Add flour to make a roux, stirring constantly. Cook for 1 minute. Gradually stir in cream, chicken broth, swiss cheese, and parmesan cheese. Season to taste with salt and pepper. Garnish with parsley and serve hot over cooked pasta.

all day beef stew

2 ½ pounds	beef, cut into 1 ½" cubes
8 medium	red potatoes, quartered
8	carrots, peeled and cut into 2" chunks
1	yellow onion, peeled and diced
1	turnip, peeled and diced
1	celery rib, cut into ½ inch pieces
2	bay leaves
¼ teaspoon	black pepper
¼ teaspoon	salt
¼ teaspoon	worcestershire sauce
1 (15 ounce) can	beef broth
1 (12 ounce) can	cream of mushroom soup
½ cup	red wine

In large slow cooker, layer all ingredients, finishing with broth, soup and wine. Cook at medium heat for 8-10 hours, adding water after 4 hours if needed. Serve with green salad and loaf of crusty bread.

baked mac and cheese

¼ cup	flour
2 tablespoons	butter
2 tablespoons	vegetable oil
½ teaspoon	salt
¼ teaspoon	black pepper
¼ teaspoon	dry mustard
pinch	smoked paprika
2 ½ cups	milk
3 cups	shredded medium cheddar cheese, divided
½ cup	shredded parmesan cheese
½ cup	bread crumbs
8 ounce package	dry macaroni noodles

Preheat oven to 375 degrees. Cook macaroni according to package directions until al dente. In heavy sauce pan, combine flour, oil and butter to make a roux. Stir in seasonings. Cook for 3 minutes or until raw flour taste is gone. Add milk, whisking constantly. Bring to a boil. Remove from heat. Stir in 2 cups cheddar cheese until melted.

Spray 2 quart casserole dish with non-stick cooking spray. Stir cooked macaroni into cheese sauce. Layer half into prepared pan. Sprinkle with ½ cup reserved cheddar cheese. Repeat with second layer.

Toss together parmesan and bread crumbs. Sprinkle over macaroni and cheese. Bake in preheated oven for 20 minutes until top is golden brown.

southwestern quiche

1	unbaked 9" pie shell
1 cup	shredded cheddar cheese
½ cup	crumbled cotija cheese
1 cup	crumbled bacon
½ cup	diced green chilies
4	eggs
1 cup	heavy cream

Preheat oven to 300 degrees. In pie shell, layer half of each cheese across the bottom followed by the bacon and green chilies. Top with remaining cheeses. In mixing bowl combine eggs and cream until well mixed. Pour egg mixture carefully over top of cheeses in pie pan. Bake for 20 minutes in preheated oven. Rotate pan 180 degrees and continue to bake for another 20 minutes. Quiche should be golden brown and firm. Let stand 10-15 minutes before serving.

mediterranean quiche

1	unbaked 9" pie shell
1 cup	shredded mozzarella cheese
4 ounces	fresh goat cheese, crumbled
¼ cup	diced, sautéed red onion
½ cup	roasted red pepper strips
¼ cup	pitted kalamata olives, halved
½ cup	zucchini, halved and sliced
4	eggs
1 cup	heavy cream

Preheat oven to 300 degrees. In pie shell, sprinkle half the mozzarella, then half the goat cheese. Top with onions, peppers, olives, zucchini, then remaining cheese. In a mixing bowl combine eggs and cream until well mixed. Pour egg mixture carefully over the top of the cheeses in pie pan. Bake for 20 minutes. Rotate pan 180 degrees and continue to bake for another 20 minutes. Quiche should be golden brown and set. Let stand 10-15 minutes before serving.

white trash enchiladas

12	8" flour tortillas
4 cups	shredded chicken, cooked
1 (28 ounce) can	green enchilada sauce
1 (15 ounce) can	cream of mushroom soup
16 ounces	shredded cheddar cheese, reserving 1 cup
8 ounces	sour cream
½ cup	heavy cream
1 (4 ounce) can	diced green chilies

Preheat oven to 350 degrees. Combine chicken, enchilada sauce, soup, cheddar cheese, sour cream, heavy cream and green chilies. Reserve 1 cup of mixture. Spread ½ cup of reserved mixture on bottom of well-greased 9" x 13" casserole dish. Briefly warm flour tortillas in microwave just to soften-less than 1 minute. Divide remaining chicken mixture between flour tortillas. Roll and place in casserole dish. Top with last ½ cup of reserved chicken mixture. Bake in preheated oven for 25 minutes or until hot and bubbly. Remove from oven. Sprinkle top with reserved cheese. Continue baking until cheese is melted.

celebration waffles with fruit syrups

1½ cups	flour
1 tablespoon	baking powder
½ teaspoon	salt
1 tablespoon	sugar
2 cups	milk
2	egg yolks
2	egg whites, beaten until stiff
¼ cup	melted butter or margarine

Combine all ingredients except egg whites. Stir until just mixed. Fold in egg whites. Bake in greased hot waffle iron until golden brown. Makes approximately 6-8 waffles.

*Serve with Blackberry Syrup or Peach Syrup.
Recipes on page 102*

blackberry syrup

3 cups	fresh or frozen blackberries
¾ cup	granulated sugar
	juice of ½ lemon
½ cup	water

Combine all ingredients in a heavy bottomed sauce pan. Bring to a boil and cook, stirring for 5 minutes. Remove from heat and smash any whole berries against side of pan with spoon. Serve warm.

peach syrup

4 cups	fresh or frozen peaches peeled and sliced
1 cup	water
	juice of 1 lemon
1 cup	sugar
¼ cup	light corn syrup
1	cinnamon stick
⅛ teaspoon	almond extract

Bring all ingredients except almond extract to a boil in a heavy saucepan. Cook, stirring, for 5 minutes. Remove from heat and let stand for 10 minutes. Remove cinnamon stick. Pour into blender and puree until smooth. Stir in almond extract and serve warm.

side dishes

"One cannot think well, love well, sleep well, if one has not dined well."

– Virginia Woolf

side dishes

Potatoes Au Gratin

Cheesy Grits

Creamed Corn

Lemon Pepper Asparagus

Sweet Potato Casserole

Browned Butter Orzo

Garlic Green Beans

Baked Beans

Roasted Root Vegetables with Whiskey Sauce

Cilantro Rice

Cowboy Potatoes

Oven Roasted Tuscan Potatoes

potatoes au gratin

8	russet potatoes, peeled and cut into ¼" slices
2	yellow onions, diced
	salt and pepper, to taste
¼ cup + 2 tablespoons	butter
2 tablespoons	flour
2 cups	milk
2 cups	heavy cream
2 ½ cups	shredded cheddar cheese
½ cup	bread crumbs
½ cup	parmesan or asiago cheese

Preheat oven to 400 degrees. Toss potatoes in salt and pepper. Using the reserved ¼ cup, generously butter a 2 quart casserole dish and layer ¼ of the potatoes across the bottom. Sprinkle with ⅓ of the onions and repeat alternating layers of potatoes and onions until all of them are in the casserole dish, ending with potatoes. In a medium saucepan over medium heat, melt the remaining 2 tablespoon of butter and add the flour to make a roux. Cook for about a minute and then gradually stir in the milk and cream. Bring to a light boil and then reduce heat to very low. Gradually whisk in the cheese a little at a time so it melts thoroughly and evenly. Pour this mixture over the potatoes in the casserole dish. Mix the bread crumbs with the parmesan cheese and sprinkle in an even layer across the top. Cover dish with foil and bake for an hour. Remove foil and continue to bake for another 20-30 minutes until the top is golden brown. Let rest for about 10 minutes before cutting and serving.

cheesy grits

1 cup	coarsely ground grits
3 cups	water
	pinch of salt
2 cups	half-n-half
1 cup	shredded medium or sharp cheddar cheese
	black pepper to taste

Combine grits, water and salt in a medium saucepan and bring to a boil. Stir in the half-n-half and turn heat to low. Simmer for about 15-20 minutes or until grits are thickened and tender. While still on the heat, gradually add the cheese a little at a time so it melts evenly and thoroughly. Season with black pepper to taste and serve warm.

creamed corn

3 cups	white corn kernels, fresh or frozen
1 ½ cups	heavy cream
1 teaspoon	sugar
½ teaspoon	seasoned salt
⅛ teaspoon	white pepper
2 teaspoons	cornstarch
⅛ cup	cold water

In heavy saucepan bring corn, cream and seasonings to a boil. Cook, stirring, for 5 minutes. Dissolve cornstarch in cold water. Gradually add to corn and cream mixture. Continue cooking until mixture is thickened.

lemon pepper asparagus

1 bunch	fresh asparagus
1	lemon, halved
	salt and black pepper grinder, to taste
¼ cup	extra virgin olive oil

Preheat oven to 350 degrees. Cut the bottom 1 to 1 ½" off the asparagus stalks and spread on a cookie sheet. Squeeze the juice from the lemon over the asparagus, making sure to catch and discard any seeds or pulp. Drizzle the olive oil on top and sprinkle with salt and pepper to taste. Toss asparagus a few times to coat evenly with all the ingredients and then spread evenly on the cookie sheet. Roast for 7-10 minutes or until asparagus is bright green and tender. Serve warm as a side or appetizer.

sweet potato casserole

for topping:

1 cup	brown sugar
⅓ cup	flour
½ cup	chopped pecans
½ cup	uncooked old fashioned oats
½ teaspoon	cinnamon
¼ cup	butter, cold

Combine all ingredients in work bowl of food processor. Pulse until well combined and butter is divided throughout mixture. Set aside.

for sweet potatoes:

2 ½ cups	cooked sweet potatoes
½ cup	cooked apples
⅔ cup	granulated sugar
½ teaspoon	salt
2	eggs, beaten
1 teaspoon	vanilla
½ cup	butter, room temperature

Preheat oven to 350 degrees. Mash all ingredients together until desired consistency is reached. Spread in buttered 2 quart casserole dish. Sprinkle the surface of the sweet potatoes evenly with topping mixture. Bake for 30 minutes. Let stand 20 minutes before serving. Serve warm.

browned butter orzo

1 cup	orzo pasta
2 quarts	water
	salt to taste
2 sticks	salted butter
¼ cup	white wine

Salt the water until it tastes like the ocean. Bring to a boil and then add the pasta. Boil for 8-10 minutes, stirring occasionally, until the pasta reaches al dente. Strain and run under cold water until all the pasta is cool then set it aside. Cook the butter in a small saucepan over low heat for about 15 minutes or until it starts to smell nutty and the milk solids have turned brown and sunk to the bottom. Remove from heat and have a lid ready for when you add the white wine. The wine will bubble and burst when it is added to the hot butter so the pot needs to be covered immediately after adding wine to avoid burns. Pour the wine in very quickly and instantly cover the pot with the lid and hold it there until you can hear the bubbling has stopped. Strain the butter through cheesecloth or a coffee filter to remove the milk solids. Pour the sauce into a medium saucepan with the orzo and toss on medium heat until thoroughly warmed. Serve with fish or chicken.

garlic green beans

1 pound	fresh green beans, ends trimmed
2 tablespoons	extra virgin olive oil
4 cloves	garlic, minced
	salt and black pepper, to taste

Bring a medium pot of water to a boil and add green beans. Cook the beans until they turn bright green and are slightly tender then drain them and rinse under cold water to stop them from overcooking. Heat the olive oil on medium heat and add the garlic. Cook for a few moments and then add the green beans. Toss or stir to coat the green beans and cook until warmed thoroughly. Serve warm as a side or an appetizer.

baked beans

1 tablespoon	vegetable or canola oil
4 strips	uncooked bacon, chopped
1	yellow onion, diced
1 (12 ounce) bottle	dark beer
2 (15 ounce) cans	pinto beans
½ cup	brown sugar
2 tablespoons	molasses
1 teaspoon	chili powder
	salt and cayenne pepper, to taste

In a stockpot, heat the oil over medium heat and add the bacon. Cook until it starts to get crispy and then add the onion. Cook the onion until it is translucent and then deglaze the pot with the beer. Bring the beer to a boil and then turn the heat to low. Simmer for a few minutes or until the alcohol has been cooked out. Add the pinto beans, brown sugar, and molasses. Bring the pot to a boil and then reduce the heat to low. Simmer for at least two hours or until the beans are tender. Add salt and cayenne pepper to taste. Serve warm with barbeque meat and Spicy Corn muffins recipe from page 137.

roasted root vegetables with whisky sauce

1	white onion, cut into wedges
2	parsnips, peeled and cut into 1 ½" chunks
5	carrots, peeled and cut into 1 ½" chunks
1 ½ cups	yukon gold potatoes, quartered
1 ½ cups	yams or sweet potatoes, peeled and cut into 1 ½" chunks
1 cup	acorn or butternut squash, peeled and cubed
2 tablespoons	olive oil
½ cup	butter, softened
2 tablespoons	whiskey
¼ teaspoon	granulated garlic
	salt and pepper to taste

Preheat oven to 400 degrees. In a large mixing bowl, combine all vegetables. Toss with olive oil. Divide between 2 large cooking sheets. Bake for 25-35 minutes or until vegetables are cooked and softened, stirring halfway through cooking time. While vegetables are cooking, cream together butter, whiskey and garlic. Remove vegetables from oven and transfer to serving dish. Dot with softened butter mixture. Serve warm.

cilantro rice

1 cup	medium grain white rice
1 cup	chicken or vegetable stock
1 cup	beer
½ cup	fresh cilantro, chopped
2 teaspoons	onion powder
1 teaspoon	garlic powder
½ cup	canned green chilies

Thoroughly rinse the rice until water runs clear. Combine rice, stock, and beer in a medium saucepan and bring to a boil. Turn the heat to low and cover tightly with a lid. Simmer for 20 minutes until rice is tender and all the liquid has been absorbed. Stir in cilantro, onion powder, garlic powder, and green chilies. Garnish with fresh cilantro and serve with your favorite Mexican dishes.

cowboy potatoes

¼ cup	butter
½	yellow onion, diced
1 pound	new red potatoes, diced
¼ cup	beer

Heat the butter in a large sauté pan on medium heat. When the butter starts to foam, add the onion and cook until translucent. Add the potatoes and beer and cook about 10-15 minutes or until the potatoes are tender and the liquid has been cooked off. Serve with scrambled eggs at breakfast or as a side dish for steak.

oven roasted tuscan potatoes

1 pound	tri-color fingerling potatoes, halved lengthwise
3 tablespoons	olive oil
2 teaspoons	black pepper
2 teaspoons	onion powder
1 teaspoons	garlic powder
1 tablespoon	salt
4 sprigs	fresh rosemary

Preheat oven to 400 degrees. In a mixing bowl, drizzle the olive oil over the potatoes. Mix the pepper, onion and garlic powder in a small bowl until evenly combined. Sprinkle the seasoning mixture over the potatoes followed by the salt. Toss the potatoes until they are evenly coated in oil and seasoning. On a foil-lined and greased cookie sheet, spread the potatoes in an even layer and top with the rosemary sprigs. Bake the potatoes for 15-20 minutes or until the potatoes are easily pierced with a fork. Remove the rosemary sprigs and if a stronger rosemary flavor is desired, crumble the leaves and sprinkle over the top of the potatoes. Serve warm as a side or as an appetizer with an aioli dip.

muffins, breads & spreads

"Vegetables are a must on a diet. I suggest carrot cake, zucchini bread, and pumpkin pie."

-Jim Davis

muffins, breads

Grandma's Wheat Bread

Garlic Cheese Biscuits

Soft White Rolls

Old Fashioned White Bread

Sour Cream Muffins

Chocolate Chip Pumpkin Bread

Banana Nut Bread

Spicy Corn Muffins

& spreads

Raspberry Butter

Herbed Cream Cheese Spread

Honey Butter

grandma's wheat bread

1 cup	scalded milk
¼ cup	butter
1 tablespoon	yeast
1 teaspoon	salt
1 tablespoon	brown sugar or honey
¼ cup	white flour
1	egg, beaten
¼ cup	brown sugar or honey
3 cups	whole wheat flour, or ½ wheat, ½ white

Combine milk, butter, yeast, salt, 1 tablespoon brown sugar, and ¼ cup white flour to make a sponge. Let sit for 10 minutes to let the yeast work. Stir in egg and ¼ cup brown sugar. Stir in as much of the remaining flour as you can, and knead until fully incorporated and smooth. Let rise, covered, until doubled in size, about 1 hour. Turn out onto lightly floured surface to let it deflate. Shape and place into 2 greased and floured loaf pans 8 ½" x 4 ½" in size. Cover and let rise again until almost doubled, about 30 minutes. Bake at 350° for about 30-45 minutes. Remove from pans and let cool. Slice and serve with your favorite spread.

garlic cheese biscuits

1 tablespoon	yeast, dissolved in 2 tablespoons warm water
2 ½ cup	flour
1 tablespoon	sugar
1 ½ teaspoons	baking powder
¼ teaspoon	salt
½ cup	shortening
1 cup	buttermilk
½ cup	melted butter
¼ teaspoon	granulated garlic
½ cup	grated cheese (sharp cheddar or parmesan)

Preheat oven to 375 degrees. Combine all dry ingredients. Add cheese, then cut in shortening until small crumbs form. Combine buttermilk and yeast mixture. Stir into dry ingredients until well blended. Turn out onto floured board and knead 5-6 times. Roll or pat into rectangle. Cut biscuits into desired shape. Place on ungreased cookie sheet and let rise for 15 minutes. Bake for 10-12 minutes. Stir together butter and garlic. Immediately after removing biscuits from oven, brush with butter and garlic.

soft white rolls

4 teaspoons	active dry yeast
½ cup	lukewarm water
½ cup	sugar, divided
2 cups	warm milk
¼ cup	melted butter
2	eggs, beaten
1 teaspoon	salt
7 to 8 cups	all purpose flour

In large mixing bowl, dissolve yeast and 1 teaspoon sugar in warm water. Let stand 5 minutes. Add remaining sugar, eggs, milk, butter, salt and 5 cups of flour. Mix until smooth. Add additional flour, ½ cup at a time until dough comes away from side of the bowl. Knead dough until smooth and soft but not sticky.

Place dough in lightly greased bowl. Cover and let rise until doubled in size, about 1 hour. Punch down dough. Shape into balls about the size of a golf ball. Place in well greased baking or muffin pan. Dough should have enough room to double without being crowded. * Cover and let rise for 30 more minutes. Bake in 375 degree oven until golden on tops and bottoms, about 20 minutes. Makes about 36 rolls.

*At this point, you can refrigerate the dough until ready to bake. Remove from refrigerator and let rise until doubled. Bake as directed.

old fashioned white bread

2 tablespoons	active dry yeast
½ cup	warm water
1 ¾ cups	warm milk
2 tablespoons	honey
2 teaspoons	salt
3 tablespoons	butter, softened
5 ½ cups to 6 ½ cups	all purpose flour plus more for work surface

In a large mixing bowl sprinkle yeast over warm water. Let sit about 3 minutes to allow yeast to work. Stir in sugar, milk, salt and butter. Add 2 cups flour and beat vigorously until smooth. Gradually stir in remaining flour, 1 cup at a time, until dough pulls away from the sides of the bowl. Turn out onto lightly floured board. Knead about 5 minutes or until dough is smooth and elastic. Dough should be quite soft but not sticky. Cover loosely with plastic wrap and let rest for 20 minutes. Punch dough down and divide into 2 equal pieces and shape into loaves. Place loaves in 2 greased and floured 8 ½" x 4 ½" loaf pans. Spray tops of dough lightly with non-stick cooking spray. Cover loosely with plastic wrap.

Place pans in refrigerator for 2 – 24 hours. When ready to bake, remove from refrigerator and uncover. Let stand at room temperature for 10-15 minutes. Bake at 350 degrees for 30-35 minutes. Remove from pans, brush tops with butter and let cool. Slice and serve with your favorite spread.

sour cream muffins

2	eggs
2 cups	sugar
2 cups	sour cream
½ cup	melted butter
2 teaspoons	baking soda
pinch	baking powder
½ teaspoon	salt
3 ½ cups	flour
2 cups	fresh, frozen, or canned fruit

Preheat oven to 375 degrees, grease muffin pan, or use paper liners. Combine all wet ingredients, except fruit. In a separate bowl combine all dry ingredients. Finally fold dry into wet just until moistened then gently fold in fruit. Scoop the batter into the prepared muffin tins. Bake in preheated oven until golden and the tops spring back when lightly pressed (about 18 minutes).

chocolate chip pumpkin bread

1 cup	sugar
½ cup	brown sugar
1 cup	canned pumpkin
2	eggs
2 cups	flour
1 teaspoon	baking soda
½ teaspoon	cinnamon
½ teaspoon	pumpkin pie spice
½ cup	chopped nuts (optional)
1 cup	semi-sweet chocolate chips
¼ cup	water
½ cup	oil

Preheat oven to 350 degrees. Combine all ingredients by hand until just mixed. Pour into a 9" x 5" well-greased and floured loaf pan. Bake for 30-40 minutes or until loaf tests done. A toothpick inserted in the center of the bread should come out clean and the top of the bread should have a crack in it. Remove from pan. Cool before slicing.

banana nut bread

2 cups	all purpose flour
1 ¼ cups	pecans or walnuts, toasted and coarsely chopped* (optional)
¾ teaspoon	baking soda
½ teaspoon	salt
¾ cup	granulated sugar
3	very ripe bananas, mashed (about 1 ½ cup)
¼ cup	unsweetened greek yogurt
2	eggs
⅓ cup	butter, melted
1 teaspoon	vanilla

*Toasting will help intensify the flavor of the nuts. Place nuts in a single layer in an ungreased baking pan. Bake for about 8 minutes at 300 degrees. Nuts will be just barely fragrant when done.

Preheat oven to 350 degrees. Combine all dry ingredients in a medium mixing bowl. Combine all wet ingredients in a large mixing bowl. Stir dry ingredients into wet ingredients until just blended. Batter should still be slightly lumpy. Bake in a greased and floured 9" loaf pan for about 50 minutes or until a toothpick inserted in the center of the loaf comes out clean. Remove from pan. Cool completely before slicing.

spicy corn muffins

1 cup	cornmeal
1 cup	flour
2 tablespoons	granulated sugar
1 tablespoon	baking powder
½ teaspoon	salt
⅓ cup	butter, melted, plus more for tops of muffins
1	egg
1 cup	milk
¼ cup	fresh or frozen corn*
	*If using frozen, bring to room temperature before using
2	fresh jalapeños, seeds and stems removed and diced
⅓ cup	shredded cheddar cheese or a Mexican blend cheese

Preheat oven to 400 degrees. In a large mixing bowl, combine all ingredients. Stir by hand until barely combined. Batter should still have some lumps. Spoon into greased and floured muffin pan, filling each cup ⅔ full. Bake for 20 minutes or until toothpick inserted in muffins comes out mostly clean. While still hot, spread butter lightly over tops of muffins. Serve warm.

raspberry butter

1 pound	butter, softened
1 cup	best quality raspberry jam
½ cup	powdered sugar
½ teaspoon	vanilla
2 drops	almond extract

Cream all ingredients in food processor or with electric hand mixer until light and fluffy. Serve with warm bread, rolls or muffins.

herbed cream cheese spread

1 pound	cream cheese, softened
8 ounces	butter, softened
1 teaspoon	granulated garlic
½ teaspoon	dried parsley
¼ teaspoon	black pepper
¼ teaspoon	dried basil
¼ teaspoon	dried thyme
¼ teaspoon	dried oregano
½ cup	finely grated parmesan

Combine all ingredients in mixing bowl. Cream until light and fluffy. Serve with crackers or warm breads.

honey butter

1 pound	butter, softened
1 cup	honey
½ teaspoon	vanilla
¼ teaspoon	cinnamon

Cream all ingredients in food processor or with electric hand mixer until light and fluffy. Serve with warm bread or rolls.

beverages & cocktails

"May your glass be ever full, may the roof over your head be always strong, and may you be in heaven half an hour before the devil knows you're dead."

- Irish drinking toast

beverages

Hot Spiced Wassail

Lavender Lemonade

Old Fashioned Hot Cocoa

Minted Snowflake Hot Chocolate

Infused Ice Water

& cocktails

Blueberry Mint Spritzer

Sparkling Ginger Apple

Blood Orange Mimosa

Orient Apple Breeze

Pink Lady

hot spiced wassail

1 (12 ounce) can	orange juice concentrate, made according to package directions
1 (12 ounce) can	apple juice concentrate, made according to package directions
1 ½ cups	fresh lemon juice
4 cups	water
2 cups	sugar
10	whole cloves
10	allspice berries
3	whole cinnamon sticks

Bring water and sugar to a boil. Boil for 5 minutes. Add whole spices and remove from heat to steep. Steep for at least 1 hour and remove spices. Stir in juices. Reheat and serve warm. Makes 12-15 servings.

lavender lemonade

5 cups	water
¾ cup	granulated sugar
¾ cup	fresh lemon juice (about 6 lemons)
1 tablespoon	fresh lime juice
4 sprigs	fresh lavender

In heavy pan, bring water and sugar to a boil. Stir occasionally, for about 5 minutes or until sugar is completely dissolved. Remove from heat. Stir in remaining ingredients. Cool to room temperature. Remove lavender sprigs and chill until ready to serve. Garnish with lemon slices or wedges, and fresh lavender.

old fashioned hot cocoa

½ cup	sugar
¼ to ⅓ cup	cocoa, to taste
pinch	salt
⅓ cup	boiling water
3 ½ cups	milk
½ cup	heavy cream
½ teaspoon	vanilla

In medium sauce pan, combine sugar, cocoa and salt. Whisk to break up any lumps. Blend in boiling water. Over medium heat, stirring constantly, bring water and cocoa mixture to a boil. Stir in milk and cream. Continue stirring until cocoa comes to a simmer. Do not boil!

Simmer 2-3 minutes or until ready to serve. Remove from heat and stir in vanilla. Makes about 4 servings.

minted snowflake hot chocolate

1 cup	white chocolate chips
1 cup	heavy cream
4 cups	whole milk
½ teaspoon	vanilla
	peppermint sticks or crushed candy canes for garnish

In very heavy saucepan, combine chocolate chips and cream. Stir continually over low heat until chips are melted. Add milk and heat until desired serving temperature is reached. Remove from heat and stir in vanilla. Pour into mugs and garnish with Peppermint Sticks. Makes about 6 servings.

infused ice water

- Add slices of your favorite citrus to a pitcher of water. Try lemon, lime, or orange slices. Or combine lemon and lime… orange and lime… or all three together.

- Cucumbers are great in water, too! Slice up a large cucumber and add it to a pitcher of water… refreshing! To even further enhance the flavor, add mint!

- If you want a more intense flavor, squeeze the citrus and/or twist the herbs when you add them to your glass or pitcher.

Besides lemons, oranges, and limes, you can try adding other kinds of fruit to your glass or pitcher. Try watermelon, cantaloupe, mango, pineapple, grapefruit, or fresh berries. Most importantly, don't be afraid to try something unusual that catches your eye in the produce section, or at the farmers market. Who knows? It could be the next big hit!

cocktails

blueberry mint spritzer

2 parts	fresh lemonade
5	blueberries
1 pinch	mint, finely chopped
1 part	Perrier or club soda
2 parts	blueberry or regular vodka
	sliced whole mint leaves used as garnish on top of drink

sparkling ginger apple

1 part	cranberry-apple juice
1 part	ginger ale
2 parts	Apple Ginger Absolut

blood orange mimosa

2 parts	Italian Blood Orange soda
1 part	lemonade (optional)
2 parts	champagne
	mint or blood orange slice for garnish

cocktails

orient apple breeze

2 parts   ABSOLUT Orient Apple
2 parts   cranberry juice
1 dash   pink grapefruit Juice
           grapefruit wedge for garnish

pink lady

2 bottles   Moscato wine
1 can   frozen pink lemonade concentrate
2 liters   Sprite
1 cup   raspberries

fin

kitchen conversions

1 dash = ¹⁄₁₆ teaspoon (tsp)
1 pinch = ⅛ teaspoon (tsp)
3 teaspoons = 1 tablespoon (tbsp)
4 tablespoons = ¼ cup (c)
5 tablespoons + 1 teaspoon = ⅓ cup (c)
8 tablespoons = ½ cup (c)
12 tablespoons = ¾ cup (c)
16 tablespoons = 1 cup (c)
2 tablespoons (liquid) = 1 ounce (oz)
1 cup = 8 fluid ounces (oz)
2 cups = 1 pint
4 cups = 1 quart
4 quarts = 1 gallon
16 cups = 1 gallon

1 pound = 16 ounces (oz)
1 ounce butter = 2 tablespoons (tbsp)
1 pound butter = 2 cups (c)
1 pound flour = approximately 4 cups (c)
1 pound powdered sugar = 4 cups (c)
1 pound nuts (pecan, walnuts) = 4 ¼ cups (c)
1 pound cheese (cheddar, Swiss) = 4 cups shredded (c)

index

A
all day beef stew, 93
Appetizers, 27
    baked brie in puff pastry, 35
    baked flour tortilla chips, 38
    cherry cheese ball, 32
    dill dip, 31
    jicama and cilantro salsa, 36
    pasilla caper hummus, 42
    roasted tomato hummus, 41
    spicy artichoke dip, 30
    traditional bruschetta topping, 33
    traditional red salsa, 36
    tropical fruit salsa, 37
    trio of salsas, 36

B
baked brie in puff pastry, 35
balsamic vinaigrette, 73
baked beans, 116
baked flour tortilla chips, 38
baked mac and cheese, 94
banana cake, 14
banana nut bread, 136
Beef
    all day beef stew, 93
    busy day beef stew, 53
    old fashioned pot roast, 91
best ever cheesecake, 5
Beverages, 143
    blood orange mimosa, 155
    blueberry mint spritzer, 155
    hot spiced wassail, 147
    infused ice water, 153
    lavender lemonade, 149
    minted snowflake hot chocolate, 151
    old fashioned hot cocoa, 150
    orient apple breeze, 156
    pink lady, 156
    sparkling ginger apple, 155
blackberry syrup, 102
black bean, jicama & grilled corn salad, 71
blueberry mint spritzer, 155
blood orange mimosa, 155
Breads, 123
    baked flour tortilla chips, 38
    banana nut bread, 136
    chocolate chip pumpkin bread, 135
    garlic cheese biscuits, 127
    grandma's wheat bread, 126
    old fashioned white bread, 130
    soft white rolls, 129
    sour cream muffins, 133
    spicy corn muffins, 137
browned butter orzo, 114
busy day beef stew, 53

C
campfire trout, 82
caprese salad, 69
celebration waffles with fruit syrups, 101
Cheese
    baked brie in puff pastry, 35
    baked mac and cheese, 94
    caprese salad, 69
    cherry cheese ball, 32
    cheesy grits, 107
Chicken
    chicken mushroom alfredo, 92
    chicken pot pie, 81
    southern baked chicken, 85
    tuscan chicken, 88
    white trash enchiladas, 99
cheesy grits, 107
cherry cheese ball, 32

chicken mushroom alfredo, 92
chicken pot pie, 81
Chocolate
    chocolate chip cookies, 9
    chocolate sauce, 26
    fudge brownies, 7
    kelly's chocolate cake, 19
    chocolate fudge frosting
(kelly's favorite frosting), 11
    texas fudge cake, 22
    texas fudge frosting, 23
    waffle brownies, 12
    white chocolate coconut fudge, 24
chocolate chip cookies, 9
chocolate chip pumpkin bread, 135
chocolate fudge frosting
(kelly's favorite frosting), 11
chocolate sauce, 26
chopped salad, 70
cilantro rice, 120
cocktails, 155
    blood orange mimosa, 155
    blueberry mint spritzer, 155
    orient apple breeze, 156
    pink lady, 156
    sparkling ginger apple, 155
cowboy potatoes, 121
cranberry dressing, 72
cream cheese frosting, 15
cream of broccoli soup, 49
creamed corn, 109
creamy gravy, 86
creamy italian vinaigrette, 76
creamy ranch dressing, 75
creamy tomato soup, 47
crepe toppings, 27

D

Desserts, 1
    banana cake, 14
    best ever cheesecake, 5
    chocolate chip cookies, 9
    fudge brownies, 7
    kelly's chocolate cake, 19
    LeCroissant dessert crepes, 25
    lemon pound cake, 16
    our famous sugar cookies, 10
    texas fudge cake, 22
    vanilla cake, 21
    waffle brownies, 12
    white chocolate coconut fudge, 24
dill dip, 31
Dressings, 72
    balsamic vinaigrette, 73
    cranberry dressing, 72
    creamy italian vinaigrette, 76
    creamy ranch dressing, 75
    lemon vinaigrette, 65, 74
    raspberry poppy seed dressing, 72

E

Eggs
    mediterranean quiche, 97
    southwestern quiche, 95
Entrees, 77
    all day beef stew, 93
    baked mac and cheese, 94
    campfire trout, 82
    celebration waffles with fruit syrups, 101
    chicken mushroom alfredo, 92
    chicken pot pie, 81
    mediterranean quiche, 97
    old fashioned pot roast, 91
    pork tenderloin tacos, 87
    southern baked chicken, 85
    southwestern quiche, 95
    tuscan chicken, 88
    white trash enchiladas, 99

F

fiesta fruit salad, 63

Fish
    campfire trout, 82
    shrimp macaroni salad, 60
fudge brownies, 7
Frosting
chocolate fudge frosting
(kelly's favorite frosting), 13
cream cheese frosting, 15
lemon glaze, 17
raspberry buttercream frosting, 11
texas fudge frosting, 23

G

garlic cheese biscuits, 127
garlic green beans, 115
Glaze
    lemon glaze, 17
grandma's wheat bread, 126

H

herbed cream cheese spread, 141
honey butter, 142
hot spiced wassail, 147

I

infused ice water, 153

J

jicama and cilantro salsa, 36

K

kelly's chocolate cake, 19
chocolate fudge frosting
(kelly's favorite frosting), 13

L

lavender lemonade, 149
LeCroissant dessert crepes, 25
lemon glaze, 17
lemon pepper asparagus, 111
lemon pound cake, 15
lemon vinaigrette, 65, 74

M

Meats, see each beef, chicken, fish, pork
mediterranean quiche, 97
minted snowflake hot chocolate, 151
Muffins Breads & Spreads, 123
Muffins,
    banana nut bread, 136
    sour cream muffins, 133
    spicy corn muffins, 137

O

old fashioned hot cocoa, 150
old fashioned pot roast, 91
old fashioned white bread, 130
orient apple breeze, 156
our famous sugar cookies, 10
oven roasted tuscan potatoes, 122

P

pasilla caper hummus, 42
peach syrup, 102
pink lady, 156
Pork
    pork tenderloin tacos, 87
    potato bacon soup, 54
pork tenderloin tacos, 87
potato bacon soup, 48
potato salad with dill dressing, 67
potatoes au gratin, 106

R

raspberry butter, 138
raspberry buttercream frosting, 11
raspberry poppy seed dressing, 72
roasted root vegetables with whisky sauce, 104
roasted tomato hummus, 41
roux, 47

S

salad nicoise, 65
Salads, 55
    black bean, jicama & grilled corn salad, 71

caprese salad, 69
chopped salad, 70
fiesta fruit salad, 63
potato salad with dill dressing, 67
salad nicoise, 65
shrimp macaroni salad, 60
spinach mandarin salad, 54

Sauces
chocolate sauce, 26
vanilla brandy sauce, 26

Side Dishes, 103
baked beans, 116
browned butter orzo, 114
cheesy grits, 107
cilantro rice, 120
cowboy potatoes, 121
creamed corn, 109
garlic green beans, 115
lemon pepper asparagus, 111
oven roasted tuscan potatoes, 122
potatoes au gratin, 106
roasted root vegetables with whisky sauce, 119
sweet potato casserole, 112
slow-cooker white chicken chili, 50
soft white rolls, 129

Soups, 43
busy day beef stew, 53
cream of broccoli soup, 49
creamy tomato soup, 47
potato bacon soup, 54
slow-cooker white chicken chili, 50
sour cream muffins, 133
southern baked chicken, 85
southwestern quiche, 95
sparkling ginger apple, 155
spicy artichoke dip, 30
spicy corn muffins, 137
spinach mandarin salad, 54

Spreads
herbed cream cheese spread, 141
honey butter, 142
raspberry butter, 138
sweet potato casserole, 112

Syrups
blackberry syrup, 102
peach syrup, 102

T
texas fudge cake, 22
texas fudge frosting, 23
traditional bruschetta topping, 33
traditional red salsa, 36
trio of salsas, 36
tropical fruit salsa, 37
tuscan chicken, 88

V
vanilla brandy sauce, 26
vanilla cake, 21

Vegetable
baked beans, 116
cowboy potatoes, 121
creamed corn, 109
garlic green beans, 115
lemon pepper asparagus, 111
oven roasted tuscan potatoes, 122
potatoes au gratin, 106
roasted root vegetables with whisky sauce, 119
sweet potato casserole, 112

W
waffle brownies, 12
white chocolate coconut fudge, 24
white trash enchiladas, 99